BFI FILM CLASSICS

. . . .

Edward Buscombe
SERIES EDITOR

Cinema is a fragile medium. Many of the great classic films of the past now exist, if at all, in damaged or incomplete prints. Concerned about the deterioration in the physical state of our film heritage, the National Film Archive, a Division of the British Film Institute, has compiled a list of 360 key films in the history of the cinema. The long-term goal of the Archive is to build a collection of perfect showprints of these films, which will then be screened regularly at the Museum of the Moving Image in London in a year-round repertory.

BFI Publishing has now commissioned a series of books to stand alongside these titles. Authors, including film critics and scholars, film-makers, novelists, historians and those distinguished in the arts, have been invited to write on a film of their choice, drawn from the Archive's list. Each volume will present the author's own insights into the chosen film, together with a brief production history and a detailed filmography, notes and bibliography. The numerous illustrations have been specially made from the Archive's own prints.

With new titles published each year, the BFI Film Classics series will rapidly grow into an authoritative and highly readable guide to the great films of world cinema.

D1245582

Erich von Stroheim

BFI FILM
CLASSICS

GREED

·····················

Jonathan Rosenbaum

BFI PUBLISHING

First published in 1993 by the
BRITISH FILM INSTITUTE
21 Stephen Street, London W1P 1PL

British Library Cataloguing in Publication Data

Rosenbaum, Jonathan
    'Greed'. – (B.F.I. Film Classics Series)
    I. Title   II. Series
    791.43

    ISBN 0–85170–358–5

Designed by
Andrew Barron & Collis Clements Associates

Typesetting by
Fakenham Photosetting Limited, Norfolk

Printed in Great Britain by
The Trinity Press, Worcester

CONTENTS

. . . .

ACKNOWLEDGMENTS

This book originally took shape in 1977. Commissioned for a collection of essays edited by Raymond Bellour, *Le cinéma américain: analyses de films* (Paris: Flammarion, 1980), it was written in English as 'The Three Texts of *Greed*', translated into French by Bernard Eisenschitz, and published in the first of that collection's two volumes.

Fourteen years later I returned to this essay, which has never been published in English, and extensively revised, expanded and updated it into its present form. For invaluable assistance on this work in its original form, I am indebted to Raymond Bellour, Kevin Brownlow and Bernard Eisenschitz. For more recent help, I would like to thank Miriam Hansen and Gilberto Perez – neither of them read the manuscript but both offered helpful suggestions at separate stages – and Dominique Brun of the Cinémathèque Française.

INTRODUCTION
· ·

> Total object, complete with missing parts, instead of partial
> object. Question of degree.
>
> Samuel Beckett, 'Three Dialogues'

Greed as an unseen legend, an adaptation, a laboratory, a product, a
progenitor: each is a separate question requiring and deriving from a
different set of assumptions, actions, procedures, modes of address. To
trace all these identities on top of one another is to compose a
contradictory and unwieldly beast – the principal image of the film that
survives today after almost seventy years, squatting like a dragon in
front of an impregnable castle of myth that contemporary scholarship
will probably never succeed entirely in circumventing. At best, one can
attempt to isolate the diverse layers of the 'text' of *Greed* as we currently
understand it, and hope to avoid any fusion (or confusion) of these
layers within the terms of this analysis.

Unseen legend: an amorphous work that is rarely considered
wholly as a closed form or a fixed text, but is usually discussed only in
relation to a 'complete' or 'uncut' version that remains perpetually out
of reach. As we shall see, the difficulties faced in establishing even a
hypothetical version of this 'ideal' *Greed* with any certainty are virtually
insurmountable, but this hasn't prevented the spectre of this unfixed and
unfixable object from exerting a decisive influence on most readings of
the film. A typical example of hyperbolic inexactness can be found in
Kenneth Rexroth's afterword to the Signet edition of Frank Norris's
McTeague, the novel that *Greed* is based on:

> When Eric [sic] von Stroheim filmed *Greed*, he is said to have
> followed *McTeague* page by page, never missing a paragraph.
> We'll never know because the uncut *Greed*, greatest of all movies,
> is lost forever. But well he might, for from the moment
> McTeague awakes from his Sunday nap, the book marches on,
> page by page, with a relentless photographic veracity.[1]

By definition, it would appear that the 'greatest of all movies' would have to be unseeable as well as 'lost forever' in order to keep the myth firmly intact.

As a sign of how durable all the basic terms of Rexroth's account have become, compare the description of *Greed* given almost thirty years later in *When the Lion Roars*, a three-part history of Metro-Goldwyn-Mayer presented on Ted Turner's TNT cable channel on 29 March 1992:

> Narrator [Patrick Stewart]: '*Greed* is based on Frank Norris's best-selling book *McTeague*, and Mr Von Stroheim was determined to film each and every page of the novel from cover to cover. . . .'

> [Story editor] Samuel Marx: 'One of the oddities about it is that Von Stroheim was shooting the book, he began on page one and went right through the book. As a consequence, they had about 25 reels, maybe more, of film, and they were still shooting, and that was a terrific problem for a studio. So *Greed*, which when it was finally finished, ran about some 70 reels – or something like that, I've never known the exact amount. I've run into people who said they saw it in its entirety, [it] took three or four days, and they thought it was fabulous. But Mayer and Thalberg elected to cut it down to about 12 reels. That means that an enormous amount of film was shelved and thrown away.'

(For the record, all of Marx's figures are inexact. The longest version of *Greed* anyone has to my knowledge ever reported seeing was forty-seven reels – which could easily have been screened over a dozen hours – and the final length of the release version was ten reels.)

Adaptation. The apparent aim of Stroheim to deliver *McTeague* intact to the screen reveals another myth that is no less potent – and equally influential, to judge from the above three declarations, which are echoed in Kevin Starr's introduction to the Penguin edition of the novel: 'So cinematic did Erich von Stroheim find *McTeague* that he filmed it virtually page by page in an effort to translate Norris's epic intention to the screen.'[2] This myth of precise equivalence (*McTeague* = *Greed*) operates on at least two levels. First, *McTeague* itself is deemed so 'photographic' and cinematic in essence that Stroheim's work as adapter is made to seem more or less automatic, a straight transcription. (Starr again: '*McTeague* worked as the great silent films would soon be working – from scene to scene, take to take, each episode at once rounded in its own action and contributing to the forward movement of the plot.' 'Take', incidentally, seems used here as if it were synonymous with 'shot' rather than equivalent to 'draft' – pointing up the looseness of Starr's implicit theory of equivalence.) And second, the numerous additions to and subtractions from Norris's novel in all the known versions of *Greed* – many of which will be detailed below – are deemed inessential. Both views ignore the theoretical question of how any 'objective' film adaptation of any novel can even be imagined or conceptualised, much less realised or discussed.

Laboratory. Nevertheless, precisely because Stroheim's reading of *McTeague*, as evidenced by the published script, aspired to a certain form of exhaustiveness, the various methods employed in this adaptation still comprise, in their totality, a fascinating laboratory of experimentation and investigation into the diverse problems of film adaptation, offering a veritable encyclopedia of possible approaches.

Product. Clearly favouring some of these approaches over others, the final release version of *Greed* – the only version that survives on film today – can be viewed in two ways: first as a reading of Stroheim's reading of *McTeague*, i.e. as a condensation which is itself no less an adaptation; and secondly as an autonomous, self-sufficient work using Stroheim's original footage as raw material. There is ample evidence to support either interpretation, and perhaps the most sensible solution would be to describe the film as having a triple authorship, assignable (for purposes of convenience) to Norris, Stroheim and MGM – each author supplying a separate layer of signification, inflection and emphasis which might be defined, for purposes of analysis, as a separate text deriving from a different mode of production.

Progenitor. To consider *Greed* as an exemplary influence and crucial reference point for subsequent film-makers, producers and critics, either as a warning or as a positive model, we need to refer to a fourth text which consists of a highly selective (that is, edited) conflation of the preceding four categories – unseen legend, adaptation, laboratory, product – as it has come down to us through contemporary reviews and news stories, film history and criticism. A wobbly construct at best, this synthetic accretion of critical and mythical attributes is probably the *Greed* that most of us know, but one can argue that it bears no more than a passing resemblance to the other three texts of *Greed* (Norris, Stroheim and MGM) that we propose to consider.

In so far as these four texts can be seen in temporal succession, it is ironically only those ascribable to Norris, MGM and the public at large – the beginning and end products – that can be fixed with any precision or certainty, or studied in their virtual entirety. Stroheim's *Greed*, the text that most celebrated, is also the one that is least known or knowable today, existing only as a series of hypotheses.

Judging from many of Stroheim's own statements, it appears that he regarded the film – at least in retrospect, and in public – as an act or gesture or idea (or a series of acts or gestures or ideas) more than as a material object, and subsequent accounts of the film by others have usually adopted this romantic bias, preferring to stress the heroic image of Stroheim *over* the unheroic image of the film's characters, and the invisible acts of the former over the visible acts of the latter.

This conception testifies in more ways than one to the strength of Stroheim in imposing a particular artistic persona, a persona that continues to guide and determine most readings of his work while informing our more general mythical image of the powerful director as fanatical perfectionist. Significantly, this latter image, whether applied to Stroheim or to subsequent martyr figures such as Orson Welles, has often paradoxically served the self-protective interests of the film industry far more than those of the artistic film-maker. (The sense of both Stroheim and Welles that one usually acquires from their former actors and crew members is considerably at odds with the more 'tyrannical' image conjured up by their angry encounters with producers and other studio executives.) From this standpoint, it perhaps shouldn't be considered too surprising that, when actor Richard Dreyfuss solemnly presented an Irving Thalberg Award to Steven Spielberg at an Oscar ceremony in the early 80s, he praised Thalberg's 'courage' in defying Stroheim – the implication being that it was correct and even exemplary, from the standpoint of Hollywood in the 80s as well as Hollywood in the 20s, to have *Foolish Wives* and *Greed*, probably Stroheim's two greatest works, irreparably slashed to pieces, if only to show the world who was boss. (One cannot imagine the Academy of

Motion Picture Arts and Sciences ever conceiving of an Erich von
Stroheim Award.)

A statement of Stroheim's printed in the Lorrimer edition of his
Greed script is highly characteristic:

> I had graduated from the D. W. Griffith school of film-making
> and intended to go the Master one better as regards film realism.
> In real cities, not corners of them designed by Cedric Gibbons or
> Richard Days, but in real tree-bordered boulevards, with real
> street-cars, buses and automobiles, through real winding alleys,
> with real dirt and foulness, in the gutters as well as in real castles
> and palaces. I was going to people my scenes with real men,
> women and children, as we meet them every day in real life. I was
> going to dress them as they actually dressed in life, in bad as
> well as in good taste, clean and dirty, faultless and ragged, but
> without exaggeration, without modification, and without the then
> currently popular concession to the conventions of the stage and
> screen.[3]

Von Stroheim at the time of *Greed*

Some of us may smile today at phrases like 'without exaggeration', but the fact remains that our image of Stroheim as a director continues to be remarkably close to the one conjured up in statements such as this one. It is an image of an obsessive and uncompromising stickler for details, inextricably tied to many of his villainous roles as an actor, an image that was used both to promote and to disparage his work – often simultaneously – when he was still alive: 'He's going to make you *hate him*! even if it takes a million dollars of our money to do it!' boasted Universal of *Foolish Wives* in 1920, and the following year a gigantic electric sign spreading across three storeys of the Astor Hotel in New York's Times Square weekly announced the film's production costs to date. Perhaps the most extreme expression of this image occurs in George Archainbaud's *The Lost Squadron* (1932), where Stroheim, playing mad film director 'Arthur von Furst', sends movie stunt pilots to their deaths in the interests of achieving screen 'realism'. It is an image that frequently and obviously confuses Stroheim's Belasco-like compulsion to impose realistic details on the sets and locations of his films – often for the benefit of his own imagination and that of his actors – with his desire to convince *spectators* that what they are watching is real; and various accounts of Stroheim's production behaviour suggest that he shared some of this confusion himself.

In the analysis that follows, some attempt will be made to keep the four texts of *Greed* separate. While etiquette requires me to give a privileged status to the MGM text – the film text that this critical study is supposed to explore – I hope it will eventually be seen that a proper consideration of this text cannot be carried out without a comprehensive understanding of the other three texts as well.

First, a brief synopsis of the MGM version:

McTeague, working at the Big Dipper gold mine in California, leaves his mother to work as a dentist's apprentice, and eventually sets up his own practice without a licence on Polk Street in San Francisco, where he befriends Marcus Schouler, who works in a nearby dog hospital. After Mac does dental work on Marcus's cousin and fiancée Trina, he begins to court her, and, with Marcus's permission, proposes marriage. On the eve of their wedding, Trina wins $5,000 in a lottery. Infuriated by his sense of loss, Marcus quarrels with Mac, and, before leaving town, informs the authorities that Mac is practising dentistry without a licence, which leads to the termination of his practice.

Trina becomes an obsessive miser, unwilling to spend a penny of her lottery winnings, and she and Mac gradually become impoverished; Mac turns to alcohol and becomes physically abusive before and after abandoning her. Working as a cleaning lady at a schoolhouse and sleeping in the back, she draws her $5,000 from the bank in gold coins and lies naked on top of them on her bed. Mac returns, murders her, seizes the money, and flees first to his mountain birthplace, then across the desert. A reward is offered for his arrest, and when Marcus receives word of this he tracks Mac down. After a protracted struggle in the salt-flats of Death Valley, Marcus handcuffs himself to Mac just before he suffers a fatal blow. Helplessly chained to Marcus's corpse under the pitiless sun, without water or transportation and a hundred miles from the nearest post, Mac sits beside the gold coins, waiting to die.

1
....

ASPECTS OF PRODUCTION: THE NORRIS TEXT

If Stroheim's career has generally been treated as a series of acts more than of works, there is little doubt that Frank Norris encouraged and elicited a similar treatment. Both men looked upon the American working-class milieu which they depicted, from a certain voyeuristic distance, and both projected a romantic self-image of sophisticated world traveller and adventurer, valuing their 'honesty' – a form of aesthetic scruple to be waged against genteel idealism – above all else.

Yet precisely because *McTeague* and *Greed* have been identified so often with Realism (a label denied by Norris, who described himself as a Naturalist), it is worth noting at the outset the peculiar relationship that Norris had with his own material. Unlike Stroheim, he never had any direct experience of poverty. On the contrary, the marked class difference between the characters of *McTeague* and Norris himself – a dilettante in Paris and loyal fraternity brother at Berkeley who wrote most of *McTeague* for a 'creative writing' course at Harvard; a Zola enthusiast whose father died a millionaire and whose mother helped to finance the publication of his first book (a feudal romance in verse inspired by Sir Walter Scott) – was undoubtedly part of his incentive for writing the novel. The lure of exoticism, which led him to travel to South Africa (1895) and Cuba (1898) in search of adventures to write about, also carried him the few blocks in San Francisco from his family's house in a nouveau riche neighbourhood on Sacramento Street to the poorer section on Polk Street where his mother did her shopping.[4]

In striking anticipation of the procedures of future film-makers, Norris scouted locations for the novel he would eventually write: the upstairs office on the corner of Polk and California that McTeague's Dental Parlors would occupy, the nearby lunch counters and saloons, Scheutzen Park in Oakland, and other sites. The Lester Norris Memorial Kindergarten – financed by his family, with his mother on the board – served as the last working address of Trina, where she is murdered by McTeague during the Christmas season; while visits to a fraternity brother at the Big Dipper Mine supplied Norris with settings that occur near the end of the novel.

Like many later film-makers, Norris's relationship to his seedy milieu was basically that of a tourist, suggesting a fixed distance that is only set in relief by the veiled personal references and in-jokes inserted into the narrative. Trina's dental appointments with McTeague coincided with the meetings of Norris's creative writing course at Harvard (the novel itself is dedicated to the teacher of that course, L. E. Gates); Norris's mother figured obliquely as one of the 'grand ladies of the kindergarten board' who put up Christmas decorations; and Norris himself made a brief Hitchcockian appearance – 'a tall, lean young man with a thick head of hair surprisingly gray, who was playing with a half-grown Great Dane puppy' – at the Big Dipper Mine towards the novel's end. Norris may have been, by his own account, a writer who believed that 'life is better than literature', but there is little question that his understanding of 'life' was formed to some extent by his experience of literature.

Clearly, the unremitting physicality of Norris's prose in *McTeague* makes it an anticipation of cinema in much the same way that, according to Eisenstein, Dickens inspired the film forms of Griffith. But it's worth adding that the novel includes an early account of cinema which bears quoting in full, as it appears to impinge directly on the author's ironic notions about the artifice and audience of his own art:

The kinetoscope fairly took their breaths away.

'What will they do next?' observed Trina, in amazement. 'Ain't that wonderful, Mac?'

McTeague was awe-struck.

'Look at that horse move his head,' he cried excitedly, quite carried away. 'Look at that cable car coming – and the man going across the street. See, here comes a truck. Well, I never in all my life! What would Marcus say to this?'

'It's all a drick!' exclaimed Mrs Sieppe, with sudden conviction. 'I ain't no fool; dot's nothun but a drick.'

'Well, of course, mamma,' exclaimed Trina; 'it's —'

But Mrs Sieppe put her head in the air.

'I'm too old to be fooled,' she persisted. 'It's a drick.'
Nothing more could be got out of her than this.[5]

One should note that Norris wrote the first nineteen chapters of *McTeague* between 1893 and 1895 while attending the University of California at Berkeley and Harvard. (One of his initial inspirations was the newspaper coverage of the violent murder in San Francisco of a kindergarten janitress by her estranged and alcoholic husband in October 1893, when Norris was a senior at Berkeley.) He wrote the last three chapters in 1897, after travels abroad to South Africa and Britain and a visit to the Big Dipper Mine to see his friend and fraternity brother Seymour Waterhouse, who worked there as a superintendent – a place he would return to sixteen months later to finish the novel.

This two-year hiatus in the writing of *McTeague* has some significance in so far as it marks a certain shift in the novel's overall literary conception. Undecided about how to conclude his story after the murder of Trina – a murder whose real-life counterpart apparently served as the novel's principal inspiration – Norris eventually arrived at a solution that sharply changes the literary cast of the novel from Naturalism to Allegory, with a radical shift of space from San Francisco to Death Valley. This suggests the hypothesis that Norris's choice of milieu – in his terms, a choice of 'life' over 'literature' – negated the possibility of a literary resolution to his plot. To arrive at this, he needed a location that was less socially determined and more abstract and symbolic, where literary associations were more readily available.

2
....
ASPECTS OF PRODUCTION: THE STROHEIM TEXT

Born on 22 September 1885 in Vienna, Erich Oswald Stroheim (his original name) was the son of Benno Stroheim, a dealer in felt, straw and feathers from Prussian Silesia who later became a hat manufacturer, and Johanna Bondy, who came from Prague; both were practising Jews and Erich had a younger brother, Bruno, born four years later. Very little is known about Erich's early years – in large part because of the mythology he spread later about his links to the Austrian aristocracy and his military experience – although Richard Koszarski reports that one of his cousins, Emil Feldmar, told biographer Denis Marion that as a private soldier 'he deserted before the end of his regulation year and … emigrated to America' in 1909 'as a result of some mysterious indiscretion.'[6]

Identifying himself upon his arrival as a Hungarian clerk, he worked in diverse menial jobs, served as a private in the New York National Guard, and moved to San Francisco around 1912, where he

ZaSu Pitts and Gibson Gowland greeted by von Stroheim upon arrival in San Francisco

met and married his first wife and wrote a play. After money problems, drink and physical abuse led to a divorce in 1914, he worked for a summer at Lake Tahoe, where he persuaded a wealthy married woman to produce his play in Los Angeles. It was a resounding flop.

Stroheim entered film in 1914 as an extra on *The Birth of a Nation*, and by the next year was acting in various pictures, including several directed by John Emerson, as well as working as military adviser. By 1918 he was playing a secondary villain in Griffith's *Hearts of the World* and the star villain in *The Heart of Humanity*. (A second, unhappy marriage during this period yielded a son, as did his third and final marriage in 1919.) Walking for miles every day to sit outside Carl Laemmle's office at Universal, he eventually persuaded the studio head to back his first feature, released as *Blind Husbands* (1919). The critical and commercial success of that film and of *The Devil's Pass Key* the following year led to Stroheim's first blockbuster, the million-dollar *Foolish Wives* (1922), and *Merry-Go-Round* (1923). On the latter film, Stroheim was charged with 'insubordination' and 'disloyalty', fired by Irving Thalberg, and replaced by Rupert Julian about half a year before the start of production on *Greed*.

It remains a matter of conjecture precisely when Stroheim first came across a copy of Norris's novel. Georges Sadoul reports that Stroheim first encountered *McTeague* around 1914, in a boarding house in Los Angeles, while working as an extra; more recently, Koszarski has written that Stroheim claimed to have first discovered the novel 'during his down-and-out days in New York',[7] which would have been at some point between late 1909 and 1912.

Whenever the discovery was made, it apparently wasn't until 1920 that Stroheim first announced the novel as a film project.[8] In the interim, an earlier, five-reel film based on the novel – *Life's Whirlpool*, directed by Barry O'Neil, and starring Holbrook Brinn and Fania Marinof – was released early in 1916. According to Koszarski, 'Reviewers of the time were disgusted by the "repelling realism" of the film and its "revolting coarseness". Complaints about McTeague biting his wife's bleeding fingers were matched only by those denouncing the profusion of close-ups.'[9] Apparently the parallels with *Greed* run even further: according to Kevin Brownlow, the final sequences were shot in Death Valley.[10] Koszarski informs us that Stroheim criticised Blinn's performance in an interview while he was filming *Greed* in San Francisco, so there seems little doubt that he was familiar with *Life's Whirlpool*. Existing stills of this lost film also suggest that it may well have exerted some influence on Stroheim's own conception, although Idwal Jones, who reported seeing a nine-hour version of *Greed* at MGM on 12 January 1924, mentioned that both he and Jack Jungmeyer, 'the only other newspaperman there', recalled the earlier film adaptation in relation to Stroheim's as 'a lurid thing, rather comical now'.

Despite these apparent similarities, one cannot find many precedents for Stroheim's script for *Greed* or his production methods. While it was certainly true that other lengthy films had been made, and many others had already been shot largely or exclusively on location, the combination of these factors with the support of a large studio, a large budget and the obsessiveness of Stroheim's working methods made the project unusually daring and experimental, and one that was described as such in the current press.

One of the enduring mysteries about the project remains the fact that Goldwyn Company executives Frank Godsol and Abe Lehr actually approved Stroheim's 'final' script, drafted in San Francisco between January and March 1923, and virtually doubled the original budget (from \$175,000 to \$347,000) before shooting began. According to Koszarski, both men 'had little aptitude for filmmaking', and despite Stroheim's reputation for massive expenditures they were apparently swayed by the force of his enthusiasm. Stroheim's 26-page contract, while generous, was less advantageous than the one he signed with Universal in 1920, holding him personally responsible for 'excess costs', so Godsol and Lehr may have figured that these and other 'negative inducements' would exert some influence over the proceedings.

As we have already seen in the case of Norris, whose desire for a dramatic climax with 'maximum' (therefore 'literary') resonance led him to shift his plot from a naturalistic to an allegorical space, Stroheim's own taste for pushing his conceptions to their limits often led to similarly contradictory and paradoxical results. On the surface, one could interpret his aim in using painstakingly authentic locations, costumes and props, and forcing his actors to live within their parameters during the shooting, as one of many stratagems designed to break away from the artificiality of theatre ... just as Norris felt compelled to include coarse physical details in *McTeague* in an effort to escape from what he regarded as the artificiality of genteel nineteenth-century fiction.

Yet William Daniels has remarked (in an unpublished interview with Kevin Brownlow) that Stroheim's passion for crowding naturalistic detail into shots, and his refusal to compromise on camera placements once particular set-ups had been decided upon, occasionally led him to have walls torn down in his 'natural' locations in order to make room for the camera. Inevitably, this procedure – and the absence of reverse angles that it necessitates – leads, willy-nilly, to the artificially missing 'fourth wall' of the stage, and there are moments throughout the release version of *Greed* when theatre becomes one of Stroheim's central resources for articulating his 'documentary' realism. Perhaps the most striking of these moments is the long-shot that concludes the sequence of McTeague and Trina's wedding night: after the camera pulls back frontally from Trina in tears, just past the bedroom's threshold, McTeague draws a curtain that blocks the spectator's view of Trina, himself and the marriage bed. Occurring just two sequences short of the conclusion of Part One of *Greed* (as designated in the published script) and comprising our last glimpses of McTeague and Trina in this section, this climax constitutes a 'curtain closer' in more ways than one.

Another paradox came about through Stroheim's updating of the plot from the last years of the nineteenth century to 1908 and afterwards – coinciding roughly with the period of his own first years in America – coupled with the fact that he shot the film in 1923. The consequence of this is a series of overlapping temporal layers in single scenes: the major characters dressed in clothes of the 1890s, extras in crowd scenes wearing clothes of the 1920s, and the stated time of most of the action falling almost exactly between these two periods. To some degree, Stroheim was able to minimise these contradictions by eliminating cars from scenes shot on Polk Street and restricting himself as much as possible to buildings that were contemporaneous with Norris. At the same time, the apparent invisibility of these anachronisms to audiences in 1924 and 1925, judging from the absence of any remarks about them in contemporary reviews, can probably be explained only by the psychological force of Stroheim's direction and its

The fourth wall: 'McTeague draws a curtain that blocks the
spectator's view'

capacity to distract viewers from these details. Viewed materially, these anachronisms strikingly anticipate the historical 'palimpsests' made since the 1960s by Jean-Marie Straub and Danièle Huillet – films where texts and costumes anchored to specific historical periods are allowed to rub shoulders with modern settings.

The shooting of *Greed*, which took place between 13 March and 6 October 1923, yielded 446,103 feet of negative, by far the most footage shot by Stroheim on any of his features. (By contrast, he shot approximately 326,000 feet for *Foolish Wives*, and about 200,000 feet for *The Wedding March*.) Editing began immediately afterwards, and ended with a rough cut in early 1924. But it is here that one finds oneself blocked from establishing any 'definitive' *Greed* – any 'complete' or 'uncut' version that stands clearly and unambiguously apart from the others – because of the absence of any uniformity of length in the diverse accounts given of four or five successive versions.

Restricting oneself only to eyewitness reports of those who describe seeing 'complete' versions, Jean Bertin cites an initial version of forty-seven reels that was later reduced to forty-two, Harry Carr describes watching a forty-five reel version between 10.30 a.m. and 8.00 p.m., Idwal Jones speaks of forty-two reels lasting from 10.00 a.m. to 7.00 p.m., and Paul Ivano recounts seeing an eight-hour version.[11] Conceivably, the last three of these accounts – or perhaps just the middle two – could refer to the same version, and the variations in numbers of reels and playing times could simply come from faulty memories. This hypothesis is indirectly supported by Stroheim himself, in a letter to Peter Noble: 'Only twelve men saw the picture in its original 42 reels,' he writes, and the only two names he cites are those of Carr and Jones.[12]

If we turn to descriptions of subsequent versions by various film historians, there is equal variation concerning lengths and running times, although less doubt that Stroheim had reduced the film to somewhere between twenty-two and twenty-eight reels by 18 March. Most of the earlier variations can undoubtedly be accounted for by the fact that Stroheim probably continued to tinker with the rough cut between separate screenings, but this likely hypothesis throws further doubt on which cut, if any, deserves the privileged status of a definitive edition. (The fact that Stroheim settled on forty-two reels when he wrote to Noble in 1947 or 1948, nearly a quarter of a century after the fact, doesn't necessarily mean that this was his preferred version in 1924.) Assuming, for instance, that the version seen by Bertin constituted the rawest of rough cuts, one could conclude that the forty-two reels version came afterwards, to be followed by two or more 'compromise' versions edited in an attempt to meet the studio's demands. But to settle even on this hypothesis is already to assume a great deal: not only that the version that Bertin saw was pre-definitive, but that, among all the subsequent versions, Stroheim necessarily preferred the longer cuts to the shorter ones.

As for the later variations in Stroheim's own final reduction of the film, this is no doubt ascribable to approximate memories and studio records. (The studio files cite twenty-two reels, but Grant Whytock, the ultimate recipient of this version, recalls receiving twenty-six or twenty-eight.) This latter version was completed only about three weeks before the Goldwyn Company merged with Marcus Loew's Metro Pictures Corporation on 10 April 1924, thereby becoming Metro-Goldwyn-Mayer and placing the dreaded Irving Thalberg (who had been responsible for the decimation of *Foolish Wives* at Universal) as the new head of production. Realising the potential problems he faced, Stroheim shipped his version to his friend Rex Ingram, another MGM director, in New York. Ingram turned this version over to his editor, Grant Whytock, who had edited Stroheim's *The Devil's Pass Key*, and Whytock developed a plan for a two-part version of fifteen reels (eighteen according to Stroheim in a 1948 letter to Noble) which he proceeded to edit. (The only major subplot eliminated in this version was the one involving the junk dealer Zerkow.) Despite many favourable reactions to this version in New York, approval was held back, and the picture was turned over to a studio editor on the West Coast – either Joseph W. Farnham or Arthur Ripley – who turned out the ten-reel version that was eventually released.[13]

Two published attempts to reconstruct the 'complete' *Greed* should be cited here; both foreground the basic materials available as well as their ultimate inadequacy. The first and most important of these has actually appeared in three separate forms: a so-called 'definitive script' identified as Stroheim's personal copy and published by the Cinémathèque de Belgique in 1958; an earlier and longer version copy-edited by Joel W. Finler, with annotations indicating differences between the script and the released film, published in Britain (Lorrimer, 1972); and a cutting continuity of the release version in French with a summary of scenes eliminated either during the shooting or at different stages of the editing, prepared by Jacques-G. Perret and published in *L'Avant-Scène du Cinéma* (no. 83–4, July–September 1968). The second attempt, confidently entitled *The Complete Greed* and published in the United States (New York: Dutton, 1972) is essentially a collection of 348 stills and 52 production stills assembled and annotated by Herman G. Weinberg.

Unfortunately, the version published in Belgium, which may well have served as Stroheim's shooting script and which Finler roughly calculates would have been about an hour shorter than the version he edited, is not easily come by nowadays. After this study was all but completed, I had an opportunity, thanks to the assistance of Dominique Brun, to examine briefly both the original manuscript and the published version at the Cinémathèque Française, which enabled me to correct a few misunderstandings about the lengthier version – the basis of the analysis that follows – without clarifying to what degree the shorter version corresponds precisely to what Stroheim actually shot. Another factor which has to be taken into account is the fact that several scenes were shot which apparently don't appear in either published version. Koszarski cites such scenes as Maria Macapa's burial of a pet raven in the yard outside Zerkow's shack and a comic incident in which McTeague bets Marcus he can't put a cueball in his mouth (both incidents in the novel), as well as a planned scene of the funeral of McTeague's mother (not part of the novel) that apparently wasn't shot only because a Goldwyn executive who was present insisted that it would cost too much money. (Weinberg, moreover, includes four stills illustrating a nightmare of Trina's about Maria after her murder that is alluded to but not shown or recounted in the Lorrimer version.) Because it is impossible, apart from the partial evidence of production stills and news stories, to determine how many such scenes were added – and how many scenes in the published versions were never shot – the published scripts, while invaluable, clearly offer only an approximate, incomplete and ambiguous glimpse at what the initial rough cuts of *Greed* were like.

Regarding Weinberg's collection of stills, it is of course a commonplace of historical research that stills are seldom an infallible guide to what was shot and/or included in a film. Moreover, the credibility of Weinberg's claim of 'completeness' is seriously weakened if one considers the substantial portions of even the ten-reel release version of *Greed* that are unrepresented in his book, and an occasionally scrambled arrangement of the stills that is at odds with the chronology of the script. At best, we learn something more from this book about what the characters and settings looked like, but very little about the narrative construction, and next to nothing about the *mise en scène*.

The time has come nevertheless to compare the contents of Stroheim's published script with Norris's novel, since it is only through this juxtaposition that certain features of the 'ungraspable' Stroheim text – and, even more, Stroheim's pre-production designs and intentions – can be discerned. (A comparison of this script and the release version will follow in the next section.)

The first important thing to note is that an enormous amount of material has been added by Stroheim, particularly in the opening scenes. Nearly a fifth of the plot (a quarter in the later version of the script – 69 out of 277 manuscript pages) transpires before one arrives at McTeague eating his Sunday dinner at the car conductors' coffee joint, the subject of the novel's opening sentence. Mac's life prior to his arrival in San Francisco, which takes up about a quarter of this prologue – over twenty-four pages in the published script – comprises an elaboration of only two shortish paragraphs in the novel.

A brilliantly designed and extended sequence that comes four pages later in the published script, and encompasses about thirty pages more, introduces all the other major characters in the film on a 'typical' Saturday, the day that precedes the novel's opening. What seems most remarkable about this sequence today is its relative lack of plot (which is undoubtedly why the entirety of this sequence is missing from the release version). It follows a five-year interval after Mac has parted company with an older dentist who has trained him, and moved into a house on the corner of Laguna and Hayes Streets in San Francisco to establish his own Dental Parlors. At this point in the narrative, he has encountered Marcus Schouler, who lives in the same building, only briefly, and the latter hasn't even been identified yet by name.

The Saturday sequence, after an intertitle ('The poor man's inspiration – Saturday!'), opens with Old Grannis at his dog hospital, shortly joined by Marcus, his assistant. After Marcus kills a puppy off-screen with chloroform and Grannis pays Zerkow, a junkman, to dispose of it, Grannis proceeds to a second-hand bookseller, collects a stack of magazines and continues home – the same building where Mac and Marcus live – where he has a brief, embarrassing encounter with Miss Baker, an old maid who returns at the same time. We are also introduced to Maria Macapa, the building's maid, who observes them both. After some cross-cutting between Grannis and Miss Baker, who occupy adjacent rooms and shyly listen for each other's movements, Mac receives a visit from Marcus, who shows him a new necktie he has bought and then, saying that he has to get ready to meet his cousin Trina at the ferry, goes to his room and undresses. Mac leaves to have lunch, and the focus shifts back to Marcus on his way to the bathroom in his underwear, embarrassing Miss Baker en route.

The sequence continues in this casual, expositional manner, cross-cutting between Marcus, Grannis, Miss Baker and Mac in their separate (though occasionally intersecting) activities, expanding its focus to other tenants in the building and then to Trina, selling dolls she has made to her uncle's toy store elsewhere in San Francisco (and mentioning, in passing, her date with Marcus). Mac purchases a male canary in a gilded cage, and encounters Marcus again as the latter is leaving; Marcus boards a streetcar and argues with the conductor; Trina argues with a German butcher about being overcharged for sausages; Mac hangs up the birdcage and goes out again; Marcus and Trina meet at the ferry. Then a very long scene is devoted to a visit of Maria Macapa to Zerkow, who buys various articles of junk from her and gets her to describe a set of gold dishes that she has previously claimed her family once owned.

Other subsequent events include Marcus having dinner with the Sieppe family in Oakland, Mac examining a gigantic sculpture of a gold tooth that he wants to buy eventually, and Miss Baker reading an old romantic novel while Grannis binds his magazines next door.... The point of this detailed description is to stress that, while virtually all the major characters and themes of *Greed* are presented in this section, practically nothing of any narrative consequence happens. A leisurely and very literary form of exposition that would not have seemed out of place in a nineteenth-century novel, although *McTeague* uses it very sparingly, this method suggests something quite radical for film, and not only for that period; it might even seem a bit over-extended in an Antonioni film of the 60s. Indeed, despite the narrative pretext that all the characters in this section live in the same building (except for Trina and Zerkow, who are introduced through their links with Marcus, Grannis and Maria), this sequence bears a striking resemblance to the first hour of Jacques Rivette's *Out 1: Spectre* (1972), in which several independent narrative threads are established before the spectator is allowed to see any narrative connections between them. It seems plausible that Harry Carr had this section at least partially in mind when he compared the long version of *Greed* which he saw to *Les Misérables*, and remarked, 'Episodes come along that you think have no bearing on the story, then twelve or fourteen reels later, it hits you with a crash.' (*Motion Picture Magazine*, April 1924.)

Some of Stroheim's smaller additions to the novel are also worth considering. In most cases, they can be regarded as details that intensify and enhance certain elements in the original without distorting their basic substance. The following list is representative, but by no means complete (numbers in parenthesis refer to pages in the Lorrimer edition of the script).

1. After Mac meets Trina for the first time in his Dental Parlors, he falls into an erotic reverie when she leaves, tenderly wraps her extracted tooth in a piece of newspaper and, after looking around warily (although no one else is there), places it in his waistcoat pocket. Then, 'he sits down in the operating chair. [In medium shot he] fingers the part of the right arm-brace on which Trina's hand has rested, then he turns slightly and looks at the head-rest where her head has rested. He closes his eyes and grits his teeth; with a jerk, he puts his head into the head-rest, gripping both arm-braces with his hands where her hands have lain....' (111)
2. When Mac plays his concertina for Trina on one of their dates in Oakland, Stroheim places them near a sewer-pipe and includes the following: 'Iris in on a medium shot of a dead rat and other sewage floating by in the water.' (141)

3. Chapter 5 of the novel, which describes this date, ends with Mrs Sieppe, Trina's mother, setting down a mousetrap 'with such violence that it sprung with a sharp snap'. In the script, there is a direct cut from Mac on the train home – 'with an enormous smile on his distended lips and wide eyes [striking] his mallet-like fists upon his knees, exclaiming under his breath: [intertitle] "I got her, by God!"' – to a close-up of the mousetrap accidentally closing on Trina's finger (145). A cruel and ironic foreshadowing of Mac's subsequent biting of Trina's fingers – years later, long after their marriage has deteriorated – this is one of many instances where Stroheim inserts a dark detail that 'predicts' or anticipates a subsequent turn in the plot.

4. The extraordinary wedding sequence, as described in the script, is full of pure Stroheim inventions, some of which offer further illustrations of his taste for 'bad signs' that suggest supernatural foreshadowings: Mac tripping over a door sill during the wedding procession (176); the funeral procession glimpsed through the window (178); a '[close-up] of Marcus's hands clinched angrily behind his back' towards the conclusion of the ceremony (178); Mac and Trina looking at their gifts, including the female canary that Mac gives to Trina to go with the male one in his cage (179); the Sieppe children fighting during dinner (182), and the contrast between the eating habits of the minister and the hunchbacked photographer (the latter a Stroheim creation) (183); the elaborate departure of the Sieppes at the Santa Fe railroad station after the wedding (188–9), and Zerkow's marriage proposal to Maria after this (189–90), which concludes Part One of the script.

5. Trina, with Mac on Market Street during the first months of their marriage, stops to admire diamonds and silver and gold jewellery in a shop window (198).

6. Zerkow dilutes the milk he feeds to his and Maria's baby with dirty water (205–6).

7. Some time after leaving Trina, Mac finds his and Trina's wedding picture torn in two in a trash-can near the kindergarten where Trina is working (309).

8. While Mac is murdering Trina inside the kindergarten, two policemen are periodically seen on the sidewalk outside (319–20), creating the occasion for some Griffith-like cross-cutting to generate suspense.

9. After killing Trina, Mac finds the female canary in his birdcage, dead (321).

10. Mac's torn wedding photograph crops up again in a 'Wanted' notice offering a $100 reward for his 'arrest and apprehension' (332–3). A still of this 'Wanted' notice, reproduced on page 332 of the Lorrimer script, reveals McTeague's given name, John, for the first and only time, a detail not mentioned by Norris.

Other important elements in Stroheim's 'reading' of *McTeague* involve more substantial changes in viewpoint. Perhaps the most striking of these is an appreciably greater generosity shown to most of the major characters, which can be more or less intuited from the following alterations (among others).

1. The association of Mac with his canary – a device clearly derived from Griffith – accentuates the gentle side of his character, while his brutal boast of killing a half-grown heifer, recounted in Chapter 11 of the novel, is omitted.

2. Norris notes that 'Neither Zerkow nor Maria was much affected by either the birth or the death' of their baby, while Stroheim emphasises Maria's grief over the child's death.

3. Although Zerkow remains a grotesque in the script, all verbal references to him as a Jew – a pejorative term in the novel that is used several times and is part and parcel of Norris's racist theories[14] – are eliminated. Considering the fact that Stroheim himself was a Jew – a fact unknown to virtually all his contemporaries outside Austria[15] until after his death, when Denis Marion discovered that contrary to the film-maker's own accounts he came from a bourgeois Jewish family[16] – this discretion is certainly understandable.

4. When Marcus renounces his claims on Trina to Mac at the Seals Rock Restaurant, this gesture is explicitly mocked in the novel (Chapter 4): 'The sense of his own magnanimity all at once overcame Marcus. He saw himself as another man, very noble, self-sacrificing; he stood apart and watched this second self with boundless admiration and with infinite pity. He was so good, so magnificent, so heroic, that he almost sobbed.' By omitting any conclusive evidence of these hyperbolic thoughts, Stroheim makes the gesture seem somewhat more genuine,

and it becomes touching: Marcus's finest moment (126–7).

5. Most surprising of all, in relation to Stroheim's interests, judging from the evidence of his other features, all the most direct allusions in the novel to Trina's masochism (which occur in Chapter 16) are eliminated, including an account of conversations with Maria when each of them proudly shows off bruises inflicted by their husbands.[17]

Related to these changes is a certain reticence on Stroheim's part in some of the more violent and/or unpleasant scenes. On the one hand, Mac's biting of Trina's bruised fingers is shown in detail, but in many other cases the violent or painful events are either kept off-screen (Trina vomiting, her dental operation, her eventual murder), or shown quite discreetly: when Trina finds Maria with her throat slit, the corpse is shown only in silhouette, a reflection perhaps of the expressionism that informs most of the scenes with Maria and Zerkow. In Mac's penultimate encounter with Trina, when he begs for money at her window, the scene is virtually reshaped: Mac's gesture of throwing cherry pits at the window to attract Trina's attention is omitted, and the use of shot/countershot expands the point of view of the scene from Trina's to one that assimilates the viewpoints of both characters.

If in fact we pause for a moment to compare Stroheim's *mise en scène* not only with Norris's but also with the *mise en scène* of other American directors of this period – the Griffith of *America*, the Chaplin of *A Woman of Paris*, the Lubitsch of *The Marriage Circle*, the Vidor of *The Big Parade*, the De Mille of *The Ten Commandments* – what seems especially modern about Stroheim in relation to the others is the multiplicity of camera angles and vantage points on specific scenes. An excellent example of this is the night scene at Mac's Dental Parlors when Mac and the Sieppe family (including Trina) arrive and learn from various neighbours about Trina winning the lottery. Norris conceives of the scene as a 'medley of voices', but Stroheim's varied angles on and viewpoints of the action clearly make his vision the more densely novelistic of the two. His eye for detail is also decidedly more distinctive: in the novel, the agent is merely a 'stranger' in a 'drab overcoat'; in Stroheim's script, he 'speaks with the mien of an undertaker' – an effect fully realised in the direction, which also gives him the unnecessary but indelible detail of a bandage on his cheek.

On the other hand, there are aspects of Stroheim that seem less modern and sophisticated than Norris. Perhaps the most problematical element in Stroheim's adaptation of *McTeague*, at least from a present-day vantage point, is its repeated use of certain symbolic motifs: shots of gold, 'greedy' hands, the canaries, and, framing as well as punctuating the entire wedding sequence, eight separate shots of a hand sawing wood 'against a black velvet background' (pages 175, 177, 178, 181, 183, 186 and 188 in the Lorrimer script), first seen in medium close-up, then in medium shots; the fifth, sixth and eighth of these shots bracketed by a fade-in and a fade-out.

The justification for and counterpart to these puzzling shots in the novel is two passing details in Chapter 9: '... from somewhere in the building itself came a persistent sound of sawing', and a page later, after the ceremony, a line of dialogue: ' "Did you hear that sawing going on all the time? I declare it regularly got on my nerves." ' (Less plausible is Jacques-G. Perret's assertion in a footnote to the cutting continuity in *L'Avant-Scène du Cinéma* that 'in the United States, the popular expression "sawing wood" means 'living a quiet, ordered and untroubled life." ' If this indeed is the case, the expression is an obscure one that has not survived its period, and it fails to account for the function of the sound of sawing in the novel.) Admittedly, the use of a black velvet backdrop seems to remove this image from the naturalistic context that it assumes in Norris, giving it an aura somewhat closer to the dream of Mrs Armstrong in *Blind Husbands*, Stroheim's first feature, when Steuban (Stroheim) appears menacingly against a similar backdrop. But it is not clear what symbolic meaning, if any, Stroheim had in mind.

The other examples are of course more than obvious in their meanings, which is what makes them problematical in turn. The motif of gold – the most persistent, by far, of Stroheim's symbols – was even emphasised in a contemporary print of the film that was hand-coloured, with every gold object from coins to birdcage rendered in its appropriate tint. What seems problematical about these motifs can be linked in certain respects to Eisenstein's analysis of the failure of the repeated shot of Lillian Gish rocking a cradle in *Intolerance*:

Griffith had been inspired to translate these lines of Walt Whitman,

... endlessly rocks the cradle, Uniter of Here and Hereafter

not in the structure, nor in *the harmonic recurrence of montage expressiveness*, but in *an isolated picture*, with the result that the cradle could not possibly be *abstracted into an image of eternally reborn epochs* and remained inevitably simply a *life-like cradle*, calling forth derision, surprise or vexation in the spectator.[18]

Like this shot in *Intolerance*, Stroheim's uses of symbolic inserts seems to have been drawn directly from literature. The recurrent phrase in *McTeague* about Mac's canary 'chittering in its little gilt prison' – a phrase that occurs with slight variations in many different contexts before it appears as the final words in the novel – functions with less difficulty as an encapsulation of the theme because it is smoothly laced into the movement and texture of the narrative, with no breaks in discourse or syntax. Yet in the *Greed* script, and presumably in the long versions of the film, comparable images tend to disrupt the narrative flow without adding any notable thematic expansion; they are like footnotes that say only 'op. cit.' Undoubtedly Stroheim intended them to have a rhythmic and perhaps even a musical function that partially took over the role of an author's commentary, abstracting certain aspects of the story so that they would relate more obviously to the grand theme of the work. In aspiration, at least, they point to a certain 'high style' that provides some contrast with and relief from the relentless 'low style' of the narrative proper, almost as if Stroheim, ignoring the breadth of the story in its own right, assumed that such 'high' style was necessary in order to give *Greed* the status of an epic. Indeed, if one links most of these shots with the expressionist mode of the sequences involving Zerkow and Maria, they suggest a desire to move beyond the realism and naturalism of the narrative and into some form of poetic and metaphysical delirium that the story can only suggest without expressing overtly – a philosophical vantage point on humanity as a whole that reduces the complexity of the story to the simple expounding of an unambiguous message.

The curiously dated quality of these repetitive motifs suggests that Stroheim, like Norris before him, had a capacity for creating detail that was intended to illustrate a didactic form, yet succeeded ultimately, and unwittingly, in overwhelming whatever forms the didacticism happened to take. (The same paradox can be found in much of nineteenth-century Russian fiction: Tolstoy, Gogol, Dostoevsky, etc.) Where Stroheim differs from Norris in this respect is that most of his own authorial intrusions – unlike for instance the 'foul stream of hereditary evil' which is introduced in Chapter 2 to explain McTeague's brutality ('The evil of an entire race flowed through his veins') – are more redundant than supplementary in relation to his fiction: they 'explain' nothing that the narrative hasn't already directly implied by other means. Thus they appear to remain in the script as over-determinations (indicating Stroheim's quasi-literary ambitions, which were linked, perhaps, to a close identification with Norris, signalled by the quote from Norris in the credits of *Greed*) – tokens of poetic abstraction that hover over the narrative somewhat like purple passages.

3
. . . .
ASPECTS OF PRODUCTION: MGM

They said I was crazy to do an American story. It is foolish to say that *McTeague* is American any more than *Nana* is French. They are international.... Plot is a pattern, the mechanism by which infantile minds are intrigued. It is a riddle, a puzzle, or the skeleton on which melodrama, comedies, detective stories are hung. But life, raw, immense, swirling, has no plot. Its riddle can never be solved.

Stroheim, reported by Edwin Schallert in the
Los Angeles Times during the shooting of *Greed*.[19]

Perhaps an American director would not have seen greed as a vice.

From a review of *Greed* in *Pictureplay* (25 March 1925)

Von Stroheim (seated, centre) on location in Death Valley. Seated on Stroheim's left is script clerk 'Mickey' Eva Bassette, next to her Gibson Gowland

The final reduction of *Greed* to 10,212 feet that was made at Metro-Goldwyn-Mayer can be ascribed to a combination of factors, some of them connected to changes that took place in the organisation of several production companies between the time of the film's inception and Stroheim's submittal of a version of approximately 15,000 feet, edited by Grant Whytock for Rex Ingram.

The film was initially produced by the Goldwyn Company, with which Samuel Goldwyn had by this time already mainly severed ties, after being voted out of the position of president by the company's directors on 10 March 1922, six years after he had founded it (as Samuel Goldfish) with Edgar and Archibald Selwyn. Frank Joseph Godsol, an investor Goldwyn had brought into the company in 1919, was behind this administrative *coup d'état*, and had placed Abe Lehr in charge of production. According to Richard Koszarski, 'Godsol and Lehr had little aptitude for film-making, and apparently decided to hire a whole new production staff to manage this side of the business for them.'[20] Among the others directors contracted to work for the Goldwyn Company during this period were Tod Browning, Marshall Neilan, Victor Seastrom (brought over from Sweden), Maurice Tourneur and King Vidor.

Stroheim's one-year contract, running from 15 December 1922, called for him to direct three pictures and to star in the last of them. The lengths and budgets of all three films were set down in the contract: each would run between 4,500 and 8,500 feet and cost no more than $175,000 unless the Goldwyn Company agreed to an increase. (In the case of *Greed*, they agreed to nearly double the budget to $347,000, three days after shooting started in San Francisco on 13 March 1923.) Stroheim would receive a quarter of the profits – less if he went over the stated production costs – plus a salary of $30,000 for each of the two pictures he only directed, $40,000 for the one he directed and starred in. Also according to this contract, Stroheim would have a finished work print of each feature no later than fourteen weeks after production began, and, as Koszarski quotes, 'none of the said pictures shall be of a morbid, gruesome or offensive character.'[21]

But *Greed* passed into different hands less than two months after Stroheim had completed his final editing, and by this time of course the terms of his one-year contract had long since lapsed, and Louis B.

Mayer clearly saw things differently from his predecessors. Inheriting a film that he felt little sympathy for, whose release had already been delayed over a year because all of the several edited versions had been rejected by Loew's executives, Mayer insisted that the film be reduced to ten reels. According to Stroheim, the remainder of the original negative was then burned to extract the few cents' worth of silver it contained. Whether or not this is true, it has not prevented rumours and legends of a surviving 'complete' version (all of them unconfirmed to date) which have persisted for well over half a century.

The mythical aspects of the above account, culminating in the confrontation with Mayer and the wilful (and perhaps vengeful) destruction of most of Stroheim's footage, has both influenced and to a large extent even determined the readings of *Greed* by subsequent generations, not merely as a text but also as an exemplary case, a classic model of the collision between Art and Commerce. One reason for bringing up this myth-making again is not to contest its factual basis, but to examine the extent to which both Stroheim and Mayer accepted a certain complicity in the formation of the myth. When one reads in the introduction of Thomas Quinn Curtiss's authorised biography of Stroheim that Mayer and Stroheim both later confirmed the story of their climactic confrontation in Mayer's office (Stroheim declaring at one point that all women were whores, and Mayer, feeling that his own mother had been slandered, knocking Stroheim to the floor), one can observe in retrospect that the two antagonists were actually *collaborating* in the erection of *Greed* as a mythical object, both during and after their actual struggle, with each party fulfilling his assigned role in the drama. The event screams at us like a tabloid headline, or the caption for a political cartoon: Ruthless Philistine Capitalist Flattens Defeated Artist Scapegoat.

The same myth is reflected in numerous ways in the MGM text of *Greed*, beginning – quite significantly – with the title and the credits, which should be considered as separate issues. On the matter of the film's title and who selected it, we have conflicting evidence. According to a probably apocryphal story recounted to me by the late film historian Lotte Eisner, who knew Stroheim, many cans of film labelled *McTeague* turned up in a studio storage space during the 1950s or 1960s and were summarily destroyed on the orders of executives who were unaware that the film was actually *Greed*. This story suggests that the title *Greed* was a studio afterthought, although Koszarski's Stroheim biography suggests otherwise:

> Up to now [when Stroheim was shooting the San Francisco scenes] the film had always been referred to in print as *McTeague*, although there was apparently never any intention of actually calling it that. On the Goldwyn Company records the working title was *Greedy Wives*, but no one seems to have taken that very seriously, either, and on February 20 official word came down on the film's new title: it would be called *Greed*.[22]

Koszarski cites a memo from Godsol dated 20 February to back this up, which makes Eisner's story seem even more apocryphal. But it doesn't settle the question of who thought up the final title, a question of some interest and significance if one charts the source of a couple of earlier Stroheim titles, *Blind Husbands* and *Foolish Wives*. In the case of *Blind Husbands* (1919), Stroheim's first feature, his own original title was *The Pinnacle*, which the film carried in early advertisements and press screenings. But when Universal's New York office subsequently demanded a title change, and *Blind Husbands* was selected, Stroheim was so incensed that he ran a full-page advertisement in *Motion Picture News* denouncing studio head Carl Laemmle for his commercialism. The following year, however, after the enormous commercial success of *Blind Husbands*, it was Stroheim himself, prompted by his wife, who came up with the spin-off title *Foolish Wives*.

On the basis of the above evidence, we can hazard a guess that the title *Greed* was most likely MGM's contribution. On the credits, however, the facts are even harder to pin down. If the final editing of *Greed* denied Stroheim full and final authorship, three separate titles in the credits are at pains to suggest otherwise.

The first is the quotation from Norris which appears in the film in a fictional and fanciful manner as an epigraph at the beginning of a copy of *McTeague* that is shown opening magically: 'I never truckled; I never took off the hat to Fashion and held it out for pennies. By God, I told them the truth. They liked it or they didn't like it. What had that to do with me? I told them the truth, I knew it for the truth then and I know it

"I never truckled; I never took off the hat to Fashion and held it out for pennies. By God, I told them the truth. They liked it or they didn't like it. What had that to do with me? I told them the truth; I knew it for the truth then, and I know it for the truth now."

FRANK NORRIS.

The title quoting from Frank Norris

Director's title

Dedication

for the truth now.' Clearly and unmistakably, this quotation is proffered as a reference to Stroheim's own truthfulness, although whether it is Stroheim or someone else who is proffering it is far from clear. The possibility that someone at MGM could have been acting as Stroheim's ventriloquist here is full of complex ironies, given the overall thrust of Norris's statement. ('What had that to do with me?' indeed.)

Second is the credit 'Personally directed by Erich von Stroheim', with the name itself written in the style of a personal signature as if to guarantee some further 'personal' authenticity. While the fact that Stroheim 'personally' directed all of *Greed* has never, to the best of my knowledge, seriously been in dispute – despite the fact that years later Gibson Gowland reportedly (and implausibly) claimed credit for parts of the direction – the degree to which this credit seeks to underline this fact again smacks of ambiguities and ironies. It reminds us that, however much MGM may have been opposed to Stroheim's authorship in fact, it was fully behind the *idea* of his authorship in principle, if only because the enormous amount of publicity that *Greed* had garnered prior to its release clearly made Stroheim's authorship of the film a central part of its attraction.

Finally, the film's dedication, in another separate title card, 'To my mother'. While it is difficult to imagine this intertitle, unlike the preceding two, being concocted by MGM without Stroheim's participation, it still has to be read as a dedication that was sanctioned and retained by the studio – in contrast to hundreds of shots that were not. It is also a sentiment that, quite apart from reiterating Stroheim's personal relationship to the film, suggests an unexpected kinship with Louis B. Mayer in the matter of mother worship.

Speaking more broadly, the system of narrativity that informs the film proper can be said to betray the Stroheim text principally in the terms articulated by Stroheim, perhaps with the help of Edwin Schallert, which I referred to earlier: the text has been reduced to a 'plot', a riddle that can be solved. Even if most of the Stroheim text is devoted to plot on a moment-to-moment, 'microscopic' level, the overall effect of its duration undoubtedly changes this emphasis into something much more diffuse and discontinuous, with digressions devoted to the everyday lives of the characters developing the larger movement of the plot only gradually and indirectly, in a manner less apparent to the viewer's immediate perception (such as in the Saturday sequence, the most exhaustive example in the script). In short, the principles of *accumulation*, though still much more evident in the MGM text than in most other melodramas of the period, are drastically reduced. The MGM text, to be sure, has certain diffusions and discontinuities of its own, yet these are only momentary interruptions that never threaten to abandon the trajectory of the plot as a continuity and progression of 'important events'; the spectator is not allowed to get lost in a profusion of everyday incidents. In this respect, it would be possible to argue that on a phenomenological level, the MGM text is much closer to *McTeague* than the Stroheim text is (or was): an average-length film derived from an average-length novel.

The editing of the release version of *Greed* seems to be governed fairly consistently by a few guiding principles, the most important of which appear to be the following:

1. Advancement of the plot, 'plot' being defined here as the central events which most affect the lives of Mac and Trina (and, to a lesser extent, Marcus).
2. Elimination of all characters whose actions fail to contribute significantly to the advancement of the plot: McTeague's father, Old Grannis, Miss Baker, Zerkow, and several more minor characters. (Maria Macapa is retained, but only incidentally – just long enough for her to sell Trina a lottery ticket during the latter's first visit to Mac's Dental Parlors; her incidental appearances later in this version relate only to Mac and Trina's story, not to her own.)
3. Retention of one sample apiece of most of the symbolic motifs in the Stroheim text – for example, two elongated hands playing with gold coins; an enormous hand crushing the nude figures of a man and woman; the solid gold dishes conjured up by Maria – accompanied in each case by a transposition of the shot or shots to a different place in the text. This transposition occurs even when the symbolic motifs are diagetic (contained within the narrative action): for instance, the attack of the cat on the canary in Marcus's farewell scene has been transposed from the end of that scene to the middle. More generally, any sense of symbolic motifs functioning as structuring devices of repetition is now essentially lost, except for the degree to which a motif 'repeats' a

particular theme or element in the plot; stripped to only one occurrence each, they become merely emblems of vanished structures.

4. Addition or substitution of several new intertitles not by Stroheim, either to minimise the discontinuities and ellipses caused by the massive eliminations or to make certain portions of the remaining footage more legible as self-contained narrative units. A good example of the latter strategy can be seen in two intertitles that come near the beginning of the film, neither of which can be found in the script: 'Such was McTeague' and 'Such was Mother McTeague.' It is possible, of course, that Stroheim himself added these intertitles at some stage after writing the script, but the overall principles of the Stroheim text – to the limited extent that we can say we know them – make this appear unlikely, particularly because both titles would have seemed redundant in the longer film (as they do for some viewers of the MGM text). Whether they might have been added by Stroheim or Whytock at a later stage, however, is certainly open to question (see below).

The first three of these guiding principles are changes whose traces are occasionally evident even for those unfamiliar with Stroheim's script.

Just after Trina refuses to give Mac the trolley fare when he goes out to look for a job, a medium long shot of Mac leaving the building also shows Maria pointing him out to two neighbours – a shot which produces a somewhat jarring effect by reintroducing a character who, apart from her sale of a lottery ticket to Trina and her brief subsequent appearance at a party, has not appeared elsewhere and will not appear again. Similarly, the transposition of Maria's (imagined) solid gold dishes to a scene in which Trina is shown putting money in her trunk functions like a cryptic intrusion. More generally, several critics have commented on the lack of transition between Trina as a shy newlywed and her subsequent deterioration as a crazed miser, a form of abruptness that, again, suggests even to the innocent spectator a gaping absence of some sort.

But the addition or substitution of intertitles has a more subtle and ambiguous effect. As suggested in one case above, one cannot state with any certainty that all of these changes are ascribable to the final editing done at MGM. It seems almost certain that Stroheim made modifications of his own in the intertitles over the course of shooting and editing, just as he certainly made changes in his script. But because it is impossible in most cases to determine which changes are his – and which, for that matter, might be ascribed to Grant Whytock *before* MGM took over the final editing – the changes of signification brought about by the intertitles should not be equated categorically with the separate 'voices' of Stroheim and MGM. Indeed, we have once again arrived at a problematical area of research that will probably never be clarified. In the case of Orson Welles's *The Magnificent Ambersons*, we at least have a cutting continuity of Welles's own rough cut to use as a guide in determining what changes were made in the film by RKO (a reworking that in this case also involved some new writing and reshooting of certain scenes). Unless comparable documents come to light regarding *Greed*, we shall have to proceed by guesswork and intuition.

However easy it might be, according to the standard *Greed* myth, to assume in each case a systematic perversion of the Stroheim text by the MGM text, there is no way of establishing with any certainty that some of these changes were not made, or at least inaugurated, in the earlier versions of the film edited by Stroheim and Whytock. Indeed, what seems most likely is that the MGM text bears certain traces of most or all of these preceding versions; and because each separate version undoubtedly necessitated the use of partially different intertitles to cover certain gaps, what we *may* have is a kind of palimpsest that refers back to each of the film's major editing stages, though without a skeleton key that would enable us to determine where and how each stage is represented.

The first significant difference between the Stroheim text (such as we know it, through the script) and the MGM text is the substitution of one quotation about gold for another immediately after the credits. A comparison of the two quotations is quite suggestive:

> Oh cursed lust of Gold! When for thy sake the fool
> throws up his interest in both worlds. First,
> > starves
> in this, then damn'd in that to come.   (Stroheim text)

> Gold – gold – gold – gold,
> Bright and yellow, hard and cold,
> Molten, graven, hammered, rolled,
> Hard to get and light to hold,
> Stolen, borrowed, squandered, doled.   (MGM text)

The first quotation is taken from a didactic blank-verse poem about death, 'The Grave' (1743) by Robert Blair, an English poet and clergyman (1699–1746). The second comes from 'Miss Kilmansegg: Her Moral' by Thomas Hood (1799–1845), an English poet and periodical editor chiefly known for his humorous verse and his compassion for the poor. In broad terms, the first quotation is metaphysical, religious and fatalistic, concerned less with gold itself than with the 'lust' for it. The second, for all its irony, is more concerned with conjuring up a concrete image that is reiterated like an incantation, making a fetish out of the object of this lust. The quotation in the Stroheim text, in short, assumes a pitiless overview of the human condition, while that in the MGM text expresses a viewpoint that is not incompatible with that of Trina.

The difference between these quotations is somewhat analogous, if by no means identical, to the difference between the titles *Greed* and *McTeague*, suggesting a contrast between didacticism and 'realistic presentation'. This contrast can be found in many of the added intertitles in the MGM text, which attempt to anchor, categorise and define the flow of certain events that are unlabelled in the Stroheim script. In most cases, this didacticism produces an effect of redundancy in relation to the shots preceding or following the intertitles, suggesting a distrust of the images to articulate the narrative without verbal instructions about how to read them. Apart from the examples 'Such was McTeague' and 'Such was Mother McTeague' cited above, one should also mention these further instances (numbers in parenthesis refer to the page numbers in the Lorrimer edition of the script):

> For the first time in his life Mac felt an inkling of ambition to please a woman. (110)

> His dream was gone. (120)

> The following Sunday Marcus took McTeague to the Cliff House. (123)

> Let's go over and sit on the sewer. (A line of dialogue attributed to Trina that invariably gets a laugh from modern audiences.) (141)

> Three intertitles during the wedding sequence: 'And then they viewed the gifts.' (179) 'And then for two full hours they gorged themselves.' (181) 'Then came the farewells.' (185)

> Trina's miserly attitude grew steadily through the following months ... but her brusque outbursts of affection kept her tolerable to the slow-thinking McTeague. (228)

> So Marcus had left ... left for good. Never again should they be disturbed by him. (233)

> Gold was her master ... a passion with her, a mania, a veritable mental disease. (263)

As Trina's greed grew, Mac's ambition waned ... and died. They sank lower and lower that Trina might still save from her meagre earnings. (291)

Mac's meal was eaten and finished in silence. For the first time in his life he had thoughts. (294)

The fugitive. (338)

Never in McTeague's life had sleep seemed so sweet to him. (340)

The last waterhole. (342)

Mac was headed for the very heart of Death Valley ... that horrible wilderness of which even beasts were afraid. (343)

But hatred and the greed for gold kept Marcus up ... and closer and closer he came. (344)

What these eighteen intertitles all have in common is a certain narrative surplus in relation to Stroheim's original script: expositional additions that either clarify, amplify, exaggerate, expound upon, or simply repeat the narrative information available from the images. While a few of these intertitles may add snippets of information, I have not included any of those whose principal function seems to be to summarise major events that have been deleted from the film. Collectively, these examples all suggest a certain belt-and-suspenders approach to the narrative; they underline and otherwise call attention to aspects of the characters and plot that the viewers are not trusted to discover for themselves. Although *some* of these intertitles may have been Stroheim's own additions, one suspects that their overall tendency to simplify and to editorialise (in the literary manner of an authorial voice) stems from a source that sought to 'normalise' and therefore reduce the viewer's freedom to respond to the material. Admittedly, I have no way of proving this, which is merely an instinctive guess based on my interpretation of Stroheim's work as a whole; but I can at least claim that this hypothesis is not contradicted by the limited evidence we have about the differences between the Stroheim and MGM texts.

Bridging all these changes is the implication that the narrative skeleton of the Stroheim text, which often seems a *pretext* for an obsessive accumulation of social detail, becomes the central focus of the release version of *Greed*. This implication certainly conforms to Hollywood practices when it comes to the shortening of films by artists comparable to Stroheim. Orson Welles, for instance, pointed out on many occasions that the major studio cuts made in most of his Hollywood pictures – *The Magnificent Ambersons*, *Journey into Fear*, *The Stranger*, *The Lady from Shanghai* and *Touch of Evil* – were guided by 'sticking to the plot' and deleting whatever was regarded as a digression from that plot.[23]

The elimination of three major subplots – the father McTeague, who dies in delirium from his alcoholism (thus motivating the reference to the 'foul stream of hereditary evil' affecting his son, which appears in all three texts of *Greed*); the shy, genteel romance between Miss Baker and Old Grannis; the 'courtship' and marriage of Maria and Zerkow, culminating in Zerkow murdering her – severely reduces the thematic counterpoint that infuses the Stroheim text, and incidentally removes the two most extreme instances of expressionist caricature, father McTeague and Zerkow (who, judging from stills in *The Complete Greed* as well as the Lorrimer edition of the Stroheim script, are the most grotesque figures in the Stroheim text).

The counterpoint between the contrasting couples of Grannis/Baker and Zerkow/Maria in both the Norris and Stroheim texts – reflecting gentility, innocence, tenderness and charity on the one hand, poverty, degeneration, brutality and greed on the other – undoubtedly serves to point up these qualities as they are manifested in the behaviour of Mac and Trina, who are shown as figures occupying a middle ground between the extremes represented by the other couples. Without this frame and emphasis, the extremes of Mac's tenderness/brutality and Trina's innocence/degeneration, not to mention Mac's innocence/degeneration and Trina's tenderness/brutality, are allowed to assume a greater prominence, defining certain behavioural limits that were left to others in the original version of the film.

4
....
ASPECTS OF RECEPTION AND CONSUMPTION:
THE LEGACY OF 'GREED'

As Richard Koszarski has demonstrated, the critical reception of *Greed* in the United States was little short of disastrous. Although Richard Watts Jr. in the New York *Herald Tribune* (14 December 1924) called it 'the most important picture yet produced in America', it seems that the *New York Times* nine days earlier was more typical in praising Irving Thalberg and his associate Harry Rapf for reducing the film to ten reels. And the review in *Variety Weekly* has a comparably ruthless logic:

> Never has there been a more out-and-out boxoffice flop shown on the screen than this picture. Even D. W. Griffith's rather depressing *Isn't Life Wonderful?* is a howling comedy success when compared to *Greed.* . . .
>
> True, there may be a moral, but it applies to wives only, to the effect wives should not be miserly, greedy, or money-crazed, and with it consequently intolerant of a husband's welfare.
>
> That is another count against it, that the women won't like it. Imagine any girl keeping company with a young fellow urging him to take her to see *Greed* when she knows the night that she sits through it he is going to sour on every thought that has to do with marriage!
>
> As for the men? Well, take this reviewer as an average human, possibly a little more hard-boiled than the average man that one would meet in the average small city. He had to violate the Volstead act to the extent of three shots before starting this story.[24]

Nevertheless, while the film was a commercial flop, making back only a little over a third of its estimated negative cost by 1930 ($274,828 against a total budget of $665,603), it still netted a quarter of a million dollars domestically. By contrast, it did disastrous business in the foreign market – less than $53,000.[25]

The effect that *Greed* had on Stroheim's subsequent career was almost wholly negative, at least in practical terms. His reputation as a commercially successful director was predicated exclusively on glamorous continental fare, both before and after *Greed*, and the only other Stroheim film with a deglamorised American setting – his last, *Walking Down Broadway*, released only in a mutilated and partially reshot form as *Hello, Sister!* (1933) – suffered a fate even worse than that of *Greed*, terminating his career as a director while not even creating a legend around it. (Indeed, until the 1933 film was rediscovered in the 70s, it wasn't regarded as a Stroheim work at all in most accounts of his work.) Moreover, the reports of Stroheim's intransigence in both shooting and editing, which fuelled his reputation for decades to come, only helped to seal his doom as a figure Hollywood was prepared to risk money on.

But *Greed*'s critical reputation grew substantially over the following decades. In 1952, the Festival Mondial du Film et des Beaux Arts de Belgique drew responses from sixty-three individuals in the world of film, most of them directors, about their ten favourite films. *Greed* came fifth, the first American film after Chaplin's *The Gold Rush* and *City Lights*. Among the directors who voted for *Greed* were Luchino Visconti, Orson Welles and Billy Wilder. *Greed* was again placed fifth in *Sight and Sound*'s survey, also in 1952, of sixty-three critics in Europe and the US, tying with *Le jour se lève* and *La passion de Jeanne d'Arc*; among those who voted for it were André Bazin, Lotte H. Eisner, Curtis Harrington, Penelope Houston and Gavin Lambert. When *Sight and Sound* held its second survey in 1962, with seventy critics responding, *Greed* had inched up to fourth place, tying with *Ugetsu Monogatari*. In the magazine's 1972 poll, *Greed* had slipped off the list entirely. By 1982, when 122 critics voted, it had returned to ninth place, tying with *Jules and Jim* and *The Third Man*, but in 1992, with 132 critics voting, it again made no appearance.

Three more surveys from the 1970s should be cited. When the late Jacques Ledoux of the Royal Film Archive of Belgium polled 203 American and European film specialists about 'the most important and misappreciated American films', 106 of them cited *Greed*, placing it third after *Citizen Kane* and *Sunrise*, with *Intolerance* a close fourth and *The Birth of a Nation* in fifth place. On the other hand, when the American Film Institute polled its 35,000 members about the greatest American films, *Greed* didn't even make it into the top fifty; indeed, the only films prior to 1930 that did were *The Birth of a Nation*, *Intolerance* and *The General*. Finally, when the Performing Arts Council of the University of Southern California asked a panel of producers and critics to name the fifty most significant American films, *Greed* appeared in 21st place, just behind *Casablanca* (19th) and *Fantasia* (20th) and immediately ahead of *Intolerance* (22nd) and *King Kong* (23rd).

What general conclusions can be drawn from these surveys over almost half a century? That *Greed* has always been a film mainly for specialists; that silent film becomes increasingly remote to non-specialists with every passing year; that *Greed* has also gone in and out of fashion among specialists. One should also note that the recent availability of *Greed* on video in the US, as well as a couple of Sunday-night showings on cable, makes it available again in a way that it has not been for many years, except for film students and occasional special screenings.

But problems of fashion remain regarding *Greed*, and not only in relation to the Hollywood mainstream. While Norris and Stroheim cannot be considered contemporaries in any practical sense – Norris died seven years before Stroheim first arrived in America – it is worth bearing in mind that they were born only fifteen years apart (1870 and 1885, respectively). Norris died suddenly at 32, while Stroheim was 71 when he died, over half a century later. But in one sense, both artists belonged to an artistic era that is equally removed from us – an era in which their works were regarded as being something akin to avant-garde.

A passage from a 1991 essay by Robert Ray is illuminating on this subject:

> The very idea of using the avant-garde arts as a means to knowledge may seem strange indeed, since most people associate the avant-garde simply with tactics of shock, scandal, and ridicule. But from the start, the avant-gardists thought of themselves as practicing something like science. Zola and the Impressionist painters (perhaps the first real avant-garde) often cited Claude Bernard's call for a new attitude towards knowledge, one led by an allegiance to the scientific method; and Monet, Seurat, and Degas regularly spoke of doing a kind of 'research'.

The most explicit use of the scientific attitude, however, appears with the surrealists, for whom the homonyms available in the words *expérience* (experience and experiment) and *récréation* (both fun and re-creation) are crucial.[26]

One of the many things indirectly suggested here is the degree to which Surrealism rather than Naturalism or Impressionism has become the *locus classicus* for our modern sense of the avant-garde. Moreover, despite the fact that Zola, Norris and Stroheim all used 'tactics of shock, scandal, and ridicule' and considered themselves involved in various ways in 'scientific methods' and 'research', this is far from the way that we usually regard them today, at least in relation to such touchstones of Surrealism and the avant-garde as *Entr'acte* and *Paris qui dort*, both released in the same year as *Greed*. While these two René Clair films (and *Un chien andalou* four years later) still impress us as 'modern' works, *Greed*, like *McTeague* before it, seems considerably more remote to us, an artefact still redolent of the nineteenth century.

....

A brief consideration of the echoes of the texts of *Greed* in subsequent films, and the similar echo of *Greed* as an exemplary casualty in the *readings* of subsequent films that have been extensively cut or re-edited, suggest that the legacy of *Greed* falls into two distinct categories: as mythical object and as concrete object. The remainder of this discussion will deal only with the second of these categories.

As a concrete object, the innovations and methods of *Greed* have been so thoroughly absorbed by subsequent film-makers that one can easily imagine the following shots from Stroheim's script transposed, with minor modifications, to the following films, despite the fact that less than half these shots appear in the MGM text (again, numbers in parenthesis refer to page numbers in the Lorrimer edition of the script):

The Crowd (King Vidor, 1928): 'Close-up of Trina's feet in satin slippers, standing on McTeague's feet and then slowly coming up on tiptoe until they assume the position of a toe dancer.' (188)

Le Crime de Monsieur Lange (Jean Renoir, 1935): 'Medium shot inside the bathroom. Marcus lights the instant water heater, then lights a cigar with the belly-band still on it. He sits down on a chair, puts his feet on top of the bath-tub, opens the *Saturday Evening Post* and looks through the pages. Finally he finds the story which he wants to read, with illustrations of cowboys in chaps and with lassoes.' (73)

The Magnificent Ambersons (Orson Welles, 1942): The departure of the Sieppe family on the train after the wedding of Mac and Trina, shortly before the conclusion of Part I: 'Long shot of the train as it leaves. Iris out.' (189)

To Have and Have Not (Howard Hawks, 1944): 'Big close-up of Maria with her chin in her hand, filling the whole screen. Her eyes start to gaze into space and, with a slight shaking of her head, she speaks: TITLE: "Name is 'Maria – Miranda – Macapa'." Back to close-up of her still gazing into space, still shaking her head. Suddenly, she has an after-thought and starts thinking again: TITLE: "Had a flying squirrel and let him go!"' (86) (Cf. in the Hawks film: 'You ever been stung by a dead bee?')

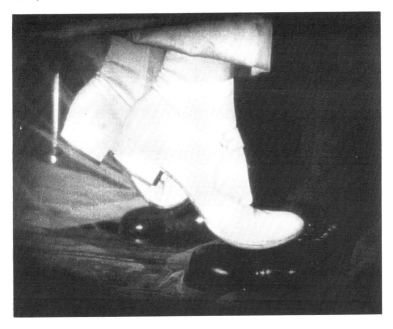

Trina's feet in satin slippers

The final showdown in Death Valley

The Treasure of the Sierra Madre (John Huston, 1948): The final showdown between Mac and Marcus over the gold in Death Valley. (344–50)

Rear Window (Alfred Hitchcock, 1954): Miss Baker, in her room, 'is putting two tea cups and saucers on the table near her.... She fills both cups with tea, and a sweet smile plays on her face as she seats herself in the rocking chair and takes her own cup.... She then looks in the direction of the second cup on the table, as if the party on the other side of the wall was going to be her party at the table. She slowly drinks her tea and smiles dreamily.' (211)

L'avventura (Michelangelo Antonioni, 1960): 'Medium shot of the couple embracing as the Overland train with its flaming headlights (hand-coloured green and red, like the eyes of an evil demon) roars past.' (143)

Les bonnes femmes (Claude Chabrol, 1960): 'All at once McTeague makes a fearful snorting noise. Trina jumps with a stifled shriek. McTeague bellows with laughter and his eyes water.' (166)

Mikey and Nicky (Elaine May, 1976): The wrestling match between Mac and Marcus: '[Marcus] speaks, spitting out words as a snake spits out venom: TITLE: "Damn you! Get off me!" Back to a medium close-up of the two men. Marcus twists his head and bites through the lobe of Mac's ear; bright red blood flows all over Mac's face and down his right side.' (215)

The examples of Renoir, Welles, Huston and May deserve further comment. In the case of Renoir, who often credited *Foolish Wives* with having a formative effect on his career and who cast Stroheim in a major role in *La grande illusion*, it is worth noting that the steps leading from Norris's view of Zola to Renoir's view of Zola (in *Nana* and *La bête humaine*) undoubtedly pass through Stroheim and MGM's views of Norris.

In the case of Welles, the taste for satirical caricature running all the way from *Citizen Kane* to *The Trial*, and from *Mr Arkadin* to *The Other Side of the Wind* (judging from certain clips of the latter that have been screened), is often supremely in the spirit of Stroheim. And if we restrict ourselves only to *The Magnificent Ambersons*, the parallels with *Greed* – as plot, as production, and as mutilated text – are especially striking. Consider, for instance, the close relationship between Mac and Trina's loss of the Dental Parlors and the ultimate fate of the Amberson mansion; the darkness of both films in charting the inexorable decline of their characters and their fortunes; the unconventional casting of both films, and the multiple problems they encountered when they exceeded their budgets. Both films are unusually close adaptations in their studio release versions, but both were originally much more creative in their additions (Stroheim mainly at the beginning of *Greed*, Welles mainly at the end of *Ambersons*) before the studios pared away this new material. Indeed, while the most obvious contrast between the films may be the differences between the respective economic and social classes they depict, which corresponds to the separate classes that Stroheim and Welles themselves came from, the scrupulousness of each film in representing its class is comparably considered, profound and dark.

While Huston's *The Treasure of the Sierra Madre* is probably the American sound film that has been compared most often to *Greed*, it is worth emphasising that this comparison usually rests on a privileging of the 'frame' of *Greed* – the quotation about gold at the beginning and the stark Death Valley conclusion – over practically everything else in the film. A more detailed analysis might draw certain parallels between the gradual unravelling of Trina and the comparable mental transformation of Humphrey Bogart's Fred C. Dobbs, but beyond this similarity it is hard to reconcile the disparate agendas and visions of the two films.

Arguably, a much closer linkage of styles and sensibilities can be found between *Greed* and Elaine May's *Mikey and Nicky*. Indeed, I have argued elsewhere that a fascinating series of temperamental, stylistic and thematic parallels can be traced between May and Stroheim throughout much of their successive oeuvres, with *A New Leaf* as May's *Blind Husbands*, *The Heartbreak Kid* her *Foolish Wives*, and *Ishtar* her equivalent to *The Merry Widow* in certain significant respects.[27] In *Mikey and Nicky*, the erosion of friendship through issues of money and sexual envy, the obsession with innocence and corruption, the grotesque stylisation of certain characters, and the tenderness lavished on irreclaimable lugs all imbue the film with a certain passion and pathos that are comparable in some respects to the emotions expressed in *Greed*.

. . . .

These instances of *Greed*'s legacy are meant to be suggestive and/or characteristic rather than exhaustive, and they apply only to textual similarities. Another reading of this legacy would look at certain 'close' adaptations of stories or novels into films (for example, Welles's *The Immortal Story* as well as *The Magnificent Ambersons*, and Huston's *Wise Blood* as well as *The Treasure of the Sierra Madre*) as applications of some of the lessons of *Greed*. From this point of view, a film like Bill Forsyth's *Housekeeping*, which has very little textual similarity to *Greed*, still has an important relationship to Stroheim's example in terms of how the film adaptation of a novel is carried out.

Film adaptations of literary works can be compared in certain ways to translations from one language to another. Both require, I think, a technique that bears a certain resemblance to Method acting, a manner of working inside rather than outside the material and of creatively *extending* the source material rather than regarding it as self-sufficient. Much as the superficial readings of *Greed* as an adaptation of *McTeague* generally speak in terms of a simple word-by-word or page-by-page transcription, superficial readings of the translation process also assume that word-by-word literalism is the most 'faithful' method of carrying out this process. Similarly, just as professional translators know that such a model is generally unworkable because of the idioms involved, the models of film adaptation are similarly ill-conceived: idioms on the page and those on the screen are too unlike one another to be thought of as mutually translatable or transferable.

In the case of Forsyth's film adaptation of Marilynne Robinson's novel, this is not merely a matter of rearranging the exposition and ending the story many years before the book does, but also of adding new details and lines of dialogue that are improvisations on elements found in the original. This is very much along the lines of the work carried out by Stroheim on Norris's novel – an act of imaginative translation, appropriation and extension rather than a simple fidelity to the *letter* of the original. By contrast, the relative textual fidelity of

Huston's *Wise Blood* to Flannery O'Connor's novel might be said to yield a work that is aesthetically and existentially *less* of an equivalent to its source: the film of an atheist based on a novel by a devout Catholic, its form of faithfulness is purely textual rather than spiritual or philosophical, and therefore arguably less a 're-creation' than a reductive transposition of events, settings and dialogue to the terms of another medium.

In closing, it should be stressed that the greatness of *Greed* should never be confused, as it has been for almost seven decades, with the simple duplication of a work of literature on film. As I hope I have demonstrated, Stroheim's brutal and passionate translation of *McTeague* into film – even according to the incomplete and ambiguous evidence of the MGM release version – is on the same level of fictional creation and imaginative density as his previous masterpiece, *Foolish Wives* (of which we also have only the fragmentary remains). It adds to our knowledge and understanding of the world with an intelligence, emotional depth and poetic complexity that belonged to Erich von Stroheim and his collaborators – only one of whom happened to be Frank Norris.

NOTES

· ·

1 Frank Norris, *McTeague* (New York and
Toronto: The New American Library, 1964),
p. 342.
2 *McTeague* (New York: Penguin Books,
1982), pp. xxxvii–viii.
3 'Dreams of Realism...' (extracts from an
unpublished article) in *Greed*, by Erich von
Stroheim, edited by Joel W. Finler (London:
Lorrimer, 1972), p. 7.
4 All the biographical data in this section is
taken from Franklin Dickerson Walker,
Frank Norris (Garden City, NY: Russell &
Russell, 1932), which remains the most
authoritative biography of Norris.
5 *McTeague* (Penguin edition), p. 105. The
kinetoscope appears as the penultimate
attraction in a vaudeville programme at the
Orpheum Theater in San Francisco.
According to Kevin Starr, the editor of this
edition, a subsequent incident at this event in
Chapter VI – August Sieppe wetting his
Little Lord Fauntleroy suit – so disturbed
contemporary reviewers of the first edition
(February 1899) that Norris was asked by
his publisher, Doubleday & McClure, to
rewrite the passage for a second printing.
Norris obliged by substituting an incident
about McTeague looking under seats for a
lost hat, an incident included in the novel's
first British edition (London: Grant Richards,
1899) and 'all subsequent editions down to
1941'.
6 Richard Koszarski, *The Man You Loved to
Hate: Erich von Stroheim and Hollywood* (New
York: Oxford University Press, 1983), p. 5.
7 Ibid., p. 117.
8 'Picture Plays and People', *New York
Times*, 25 January 1920. Cited in Koszarski's
The Man You Love to Hate.
9 Richard Koszarski, *The Rivals of D. W.
Griffith: Alternate Auteurs 1913–1918*
(Minneapolis: Walker Art Center, 1976),
p. 55.
10 I am indebted to Kevin Brownlow for
showing me portions of his unpublished
interviews with Grant Whytock, Alice Terry
(Rex Ingram's wife), Paul Ivano and William

Daniels, which I have drawn upon in this
section.
11 Bertin's description is found in Georges
Sadoul, *Histoire Générale du Cinéma*, tôme VI:
L'Art muet (Paris: Editions Denoël, 1975), p.
215; Carr's description is found in George C.
Pratt (ed.), *Spellbound in Darkness: A History of
the Silent Film* (Greenwich, NY: New York
Graphic Society, 1973), p. 332; Jones's
description is found in Thomas Quinn
Curtiss, *Von Stroheim* (New York: Random
House, 1973); and Ivano's description comes
from an unpublished interview with Kevin
Brownlow. I have been unable to find any
account of the 12 January 1924 screening by
journalist Jack Jungmeyer.
12 Included in Finler (ed.), *Greed*, p. 29.
13 Most reliable printed accounts, including
Koszarski's Stroheim biography, cite
Farnham as the editor, although according to
some of Brownlow's interviews (see note
10), Arthur Ripley carried out this task while
Farnham was put in charge of the intertitles.
14 'Norris's Jews are money-grabbers with
fat necks, their skin puffing out over their
collars. The Jew in *Vandover* tries to sell
Vandover a flawed diamond, and later when
the ship goes down he panics and dies like a
coward. Racists of the time were particularly
afraid of the Polish Jew. Madison Grant
wrote that Syrians and Egyptians had not
become Roman simply by wearing togas.
"Americans," he said, "will have a similar
experience with the Polish Jew, whose dwarf
stature, peculiar mentality and ruthless
concentration on self-interest are being
engrafted upon the stock of the nation."
Norris must have had some such comment in
mind when he created Zerkow, the Polish
Jew in *McTeague*.' William B. Dillingham,
Frank Norris: Instinct and Art (Lincoln,
Nebraska: University of Nebraska Press,
1969), pp. 77–8.
15 Apparently one exception was Orson
Welles, who described Stroheim's art as
'Jewish baroque' in a 1958 interview in
L'Express, and who claimed to Peter

Bogdanovich over ten years later that 'He was just a nice Jewish boy, and I was always on to that...' (See Welles and Bogdanovich's *This is Orson Welles*, edited by Jonathan Rosenbaum, New York: Harper Collins, 1992.)

16 See Denis Marion, 'Stroheim, the legend and the fact', *Sight and Sound*, Winter 1961–2.

17 'The psychopathology of *McTeague*,' writes Kevin Starr in his Introduction to the Penguin edition, 'so violent, so clinically presented, possesses the power to astound us and to make us wonder just how much Norris knew what he was doing, so contemporary are his insights into the more obscure regions of human behaviour. The evidence – the frank sketch of a sado-masochistic sexual relationship he published in *The Wave* in April 1897, for instance – suggests that Norris knew very well what he was doing.'

18 Sergei Eisenstein, 'Dickens, Griffith, and the Film Today', *Film Form* and *The Film Sense* (Cleveland, Ohio and New York: The World Publishing Company, 1957), p. 241.

19 Quoted in Curtiss, *Von Stroheim*, pp. 174–5.

20 Koszarski, *The Man You Loved to Hate*, p. 115.

21 Ibid., pp. 116 and 124.

22 Ibid., p. 124.

23 See for instance Welles and Bogdanovich, *This is Orson Welles*.

24 New York, 10 December 1924. Reprinted in Finler (ed.), *Greed*, pp. 31–2.

25 All these figures come from Koszarski, *The Man You Loved to Hate*, p. 173.

26 Robert Ray, 'The Avant-Garde Finds Andy Hardy', in James Naremore and Patrick Brantlinger (eds.), *Modernity and Mass Culture* (Bloomington and Indianapolis: Indiana University Press, 1991), p. 235.

27 See 'Elaine and Erich ... Two Peas in the Pod?' Calendar, *Los Angeles Times*, 14 June 1987, p. 42, and 'Are You Having Fun?', *Sight and Sound*, Spring 1990, p. 100.

CREDITS

· ·

Greed

USA
1924
Production Company
Metro-Goldwyn-Mayer
Corporation. An Erich von
Stroheim Production.
A Louis B. Mayer
Presentation
USA première
4 December 1924
UK trade show
July 1925
Producer
Erich von Stroheim
Director
Erich von Stroheim
**Screen adaptation/
scenario**
June Mathis, Erich von
Stroheim from the novel
*McTeague; a story of San
Francisco* by Frank Norris
Photography
(black and white)
Ben F. Reynolds,
William H. Daniels
Editor
Joseph W. Farnham
Settings
Cedric Gibbons
Business Manager
Ernest Traxler
Production auditor
Edward Eberle
Assistant directors
Edward Sowders,
Louis Germonprez
Titles
June Mathis
Script clerk
Eva Bessette
Additional photography
Ernest B. Schoedsack,
Paul Ivano
Assistant photographers
Walter Bader,
H. C. Van Dyke

Additional art direction
Richard Day
Stills
Warren Lynch
Props
Charles Rogers,
Frank Ybarra
Press representatives
Fritz Tidden
**Consultant on mountain
scenes**
Harold E. Henderson
10,067 ft

ZaSu Pitts
Trina Sieppe
Gibson Gowland
'Doc' McTeague
Jean Hersholt
Marcus Schouler
Dale Fuller
Maria Miranda Macapa
Tempe Pigott
Mother McTeague
Sylvia Ashton
'Mommer' Sieppe
Chester Conklin
'Popper' Sieppe
Joan Standing
Selina, Trina's cousin
Austin Jewel
August 'Owgooste' Sieppe
Oscar Gottell
Otto Gottell
Sieppe twins, Max and Moritz
Frank Hayes
Old Grannis
Fanny Midgley
Miss Baker
Hughie Mack
Mr. Heise
James F. Fulton
Sheriff
Jack McDonald
Cribbens, a prospector
Lon Poff
Lottery agent

Max Tyron
Rudolph Oelbermann
Gunther von Ritzau
*Dr. 'Painless' Potter, travelling
dentist*
Wiliam Mollenheime
Palmist
Hugh J. McCauley
Photographer
S. S. Simon
Joe Frenna, saloon keeper
William Barlow
Minister
E. 'Tiny' Jones
Mrs. Heise
Rita Revla
Mrs. Ryer
J. Aldrich Libby
Mr. Ryer
James Gibson
Deputy sheriff
Jimmy Wang
Chinese cook
Lita Chevrier
Edward Gaffney
Harold E. Henderson

Roles cut from release copy
Jack Curtis
McTeague Sr.
Florence Gibson
Hag at Mike's saloon
Cesare Gravina
Zerkow, a junkman

BIBLIOGRAPHY

Castello, G. C., Buache, F. and others, *Erich von Stroheim, Premier Plan* no. 29 (Lyon), August 1963.

Curtiss, Thomas Quinn, *Von Stroheim* (New York: Random House, 1971).

Dillingham, William B., *Frank Norris: Instinct and Art* (Lincoln, Nebraska: University of Nebraska Press, 1969).

Eisenstein, Sergei, *Film Form* and *The Film Sense* (Cleveland, Ohio and New York: The World Publishing Company, 1957).

Finler, Joel W., *Stroheim* (London: Studio Vista, 1967).

Koszarski, Richard, '*Life's Whirlpool*', in Richard Koszarski (ed.), *The Rivals of D. W. Griffith: Alternate Auteurs 1913–1918* (Minneapolis: Walker Art Center, 1976).

Koszarski, Richard, *The Man You Loved to Hate: Erich von Stroheim and Hollywood* (New York: Oxford University Press, 1983).

MacCann, Richard Dyer (ed.), *The First Film Makers* (Metuchen, NJ and London: The Scarecrow Press in association with Iowa City, IA: Image & Idea, 1989).

Marion, Denis, 'Stroheim, the legend and the fact', *Sight and Sound*, Winter 1961–2.

Norris, Frank, *McTeague: A Story of San Francisco* (New York and Toronto: The New American Library, 1964).

Norris, Frank, *McTeague: A Story of San Francisco* (critical edition edited by Donald Pizer, New York and London: W. W. Norton & Co, 1977).

Norris, Frank, *McTeague: A Story of San Francisco* (New York: Penguin Books, 1982).

Pratt, George C. (ed.), *Spellbound in Darkness: A History of the Silent Film* (Greenwich, NY: New York Graphic Society, 1973).

Ray, Robert, 'The Avant-Garde Finds Andy Hardy', in James Naremore and Patrick Brantlinger (eds.), *Modernity and Mass Culture* (Bloomington and Indianapolis: Indiana University Press, 1991).

Rosenbaum, Jonathan, 'Second Thoughts on Stroheim', *Film Comment*, May–June 1974.

Rosenbaum, Jonathan, 'Erich von Stroheim', in Richard Roud (ed.), *Cinema: A Critical Dictionary*, vol. 2 (London: Secker & Warburg, 1980).

Rosenbaum, Jonathan, 'Les trois textes de *Greed*', in Raymond Bellour (ed.), *Le cinéma américain*, tôme 1 (Paris: Flammarion, 1980).

Rosenbaum, Jonathan, 'Elaine and Erich … Two Peas in the Pod?', Calendar, *Los Angeles Times*, 14 June 1987.

Rosenbaum, Jonathan, 'Are You Having Fun?', *Sight and Sound*, Spring 1990.

Sadoul, Georges, *Histoire Générale du Cinéma*, tôme VI: *L'Art muet* (Paris: Editions Denoël, 1975).

Steinberg, Cobbett, *Reel Facts: The Movie Book of Records* (updated edition, New York: Vintage Books, 1982).

Von Stroheim, Erich, *Greed* (Brussels: Cinémathèque Royale de Belgique, 1958).

Von Stroheim, Erich, *Greed* edited by Joel W. Finler (London: Lorrimer, 1972).

Walker, Franklin Dickerson, *Frank Norris* (Garden City, NY: Russell & Russell, 1932).

Weinberg, Herman G., *The Complete GREED* (New York: E. P. Dutton & Co., 1972).

Weinberg, Herman G., *Stroheim: A Pictorial Record of His Nine Films* (New York: Dover, 1975).

Welles, Orson, and Bogdanovich, Peter, *This is Orson Welles*, edited by Jonathan Rosenbaum (New York and London: Harper Collins, 1992).